Sporting Greats

By Caryn Jenner

Project Editor Kritika Gupta
Editorial Assistant Katie Lawrence
Designer Bettina Myklebust Stovne
Art Editor Mohd Zishan
Jacket Coordinator Issy Walsh
Jacket Designer Bettina Myklebust Stovne
DTP Designers Dheeraj Singh, Mohd Rizwan
Picture Researcher Rituraj Singh
Producer, Pre-Production David Almond
Senior Producer Ena Matagic
Managing Editors Laura Gilbert, Monica Saigal
Managing Art Editor Diane Peyton Jones
Deputy Managing Art Editor Ivy Sengupta
Delhi Team Head Malavika Talukder
Creative Director Helen Senior
Publishing Director Sarah Larter

Educational Consultant Jacqueline Harris
Subject Consultant Tom Weir

First published in Great Britain in 2020 by
Dorling Kindersley Limited
80 Strand, London, WC2R 0RL

A CIP catalogue record for this book
is available from the British Library.
ISBN: 978-0-2414-1157-5

Printed and bound in China

The publisher would like to thank the following for their kind permission to reproduce their photographs:
(Key: a-above; b-below/bottom; c-centre; f-far; l-left; r-right; t-top)

1 Dreamstime.com: Alberto Grosescu (b). **3 Getty Images**: Alain Grosclaude / Agence Zoom (b). **4–5 Getty Images**: Robin Alam / Icon Sportswire. **7 Alamy Stock Photo**: Trinity Mirror / Mirrorpix. **8 Alamy Stock Photo**: James Allison / Southcreek Global / ZUMApress.com (t). **9 Getty Images**: Photo File / MLB Photos. **10 Getty Images**: Stuart Franklin. **11 Alamy Stock Photo**: Newscom (t). **13 Getty Images**: Rich Sugg / Kansas City Star / TNS. **14 Alamy Stock Photo**: Allstar Picture Library. **15 Getty Images**: David Munden / Popperfoto (b). **16 Alamy Stock Photo**: Newscom (cb). **17 Alamy Stock Photo**: Action Plus Sports Images (b). **18 Alamy Stock Photo**: Amy Sanderson / ZUMA Wire (cl). **Rex by Shutterstock**: News Pictures (br). **19 Alamy Stock Photo**: Cal Sport Media (tl); Sebastian Frej (bl). **Getty Images**: Guang Niu (cr). **21 Alamy Stock Photo**: Diane Johnson. **22–23 Getty Images**: Bruce Bennett Studios. **24–25 Dreamstime.com**: Alberto Grosescu. **26–27 Getty Images**: David Santiago / Miami Herald / TNS. **28–29 Getty Images**: VCG. **30 Getty Images**: Stuart Hannagan. **31 Getty Images**: Mike Hewitt (t). **32 Getty Images**: Matteo Ciambelli / NurPhoto (c). **33 Getty Images**: Andreas Solaro / AFP (cb); The Asahi Shimbun (t). **35 Getty Images**: Universal History Archive / Universal Images Group. **36–37 Getty Images**: Phil Cole / Getty Images Sport. **38–39 Getty Images**: Wally McNamee / Corbis Sport. **40 Getty Images**: Stephen Pond / Stringer / Getty Images Sport (t). **41 Getty Images**: Gilbert Iundt / Corbis Sport. **42–43 Getty Images**: Alexander Hassenstein / Bongarts. **43 Getty Images**: Paul Cunningham - Corbis / Corbis Sport (crb). **44 Alamy Stock Photo**: Allstar Picture Library (br); Sportsphoto (cl). **45 Alamy Stock Photo**: Allstar Picture Library (br); ITAR-TASS News Agency (tr). **Dreamstime.com**: MaxiSports (cl). **46–47 Getty Images**: Focus On Sport. **48 Getty Images**: The Asahi Shimbun. **49 Getty Images**: Elsa / Getty Images Sport (t). **50–51 Getty Images**: The Asahi Shimbun. **52 Getty Images**: Ian MacNicol / Stringer / Getty Images Sport (b). **53 Getty Images**: David Ashdown / Hulton Archive (t). **54–55 Alamy Stock Photo**: Clive Jones. **56 Getty Images**: Boston Globe (br); Alain Grosclaude / Agence Zoom (cl). **57 Dreamstime.com**: Olga Besnard (br). **Getty Images**: Sean M. Haffey / Getty Images Sport (cla). **63 Alamy Stock Photo**: Amy Sanderson / ZUMA Wire (br)

Endpaper images: *Front*: **Alamy Stock Photo**: Action Plus Sports Images; *Back*: **Alamy Stock Photo**: Action Plus Sports Images

Cover images: *Front*: **Getty Images**: Getty Images Sport / Jonathan Ferrey / Used with permission from The LeBron James Family Foundation; *Back*: **Getty Images**: Corbis Sport / Wally McNamee tr

All other images © Dorling Kindersley
For further information see: www.dkimages.com

A WORLD OF IDEAS:
SEE ALL THERE IS TO KNOW

www.dk.com

Contents

Chapter 1
Field sports

Do you enjoy playing sports? About 600 million people around the world play some type of sport.

People who play professional sports need to spend a lot of time training. Only a few will become sporting greats – the best of the best. Their success is often remembered long after they've stopped playing.

Many sports are played on the wide open spaces of a field or pitch. Sporting great Megan Rapinoe is one of many legends of the football pitch. She won an Olympic gold medal with the US Women's Soccer Team and has also won two World Cups.

Megan Rapinoe playing in a friendly match against South Africa in 2019.

Pelé is one of the world's greatest sports stars. The Brazilian footballer first played for his country at just 16 years old. At 17, he led Brazil to victory in the 1958 World Cup. The Brazilian government named Pelé a "national treasure". This means that he was loved by the whole country.

Pelé played for Brazil in four World Cups and won three of them. Pelé is the only football player to win the World Cup trophy this many times. He scored more than 1,000 goals during his career, mainly with the Brazilian club, Santos. Pelé is known around the world as one of the best football players ever.

Pelé runs with the ball during
a friendly game between Brazil
and Scotland in 1966.

Seattle Mariners player Ichiro Suzuki hits the ball. He is playing in a 2010 baseball game against the Kansas City Royals.

Ichiro Suzuki was already a baseball star in Japan when he moved to the USA. He was named Most Valuable Player (MVP) during the Major League Baseball (MLB) 2001 season. During his career, Suzuki had more than 4,000 hits. This means that he hit the ball and reached first base more than 4,000 times. In fact, Suzuki set the record for most hits in a season.

Jackie Robinson is a baseball legend.
He was the first African American player
in MLB. Robinson was named MVP in
1949. A statue of Robinson stands outside
Dodger Stadium in Los Angeles, USA,
as his team, the Brooklyn
Dodgers, moved to Los
Angeles after 1957.

Robinson poses for a
picture in his Brooklyn
Dodgers uniform. His
success inspired other
African Americans
in professional sports.

Michelle Wie has a strong swing and can hit the golf ball long distances. She's been playing golf since the age of four. Wie turned professional as a teenager. She has already won the Women's Open – one of the four major golf competitions.

Michelle Wie practising before the 2017 Solheim Cup. She played against female golfers from the USA and Europe.

Tiger Woods celebrates winning the 2019 Masters. He scored 13 under par. Par is the number of shots a golfer should need to complete a course.

So far, golfing great Tiger Woods has won 81 Professional Golf Association (PGA) tournaments. After taking a break, he was given the 2018 Comeback of the Year award. A year later, he went on to win the Masters. Woods has had a lifetime of golfing success.

National Football League (NFL) player Tom Brady joined the New England Patriots in 2000. However, he did not play much during his first season. Brady got his chance in 2001, when he led the Patriots to win the Super Bowl. The Super Bowl is the game that decides the winning team of the NFL.

As a quarterback, Brady chooses the best way for his team to score a touchdown and gain six points. Should he pass the ball or run? His skill as a quarterback has made him a sporting great.

Brady has now played for the Patriots in nine Super Bowls. He won six of them. This is the most of any American football player. Brady was also named Most Valuable Player (MVP) in four Super Bowls.

Tom Brady passes the ball during a New England Patriots vs. Kansas City Chiefs game in 2019. The Patriots won 37–31.

Wasim Akram bowls
for Pakistan in 1999.

Talented cricketer Wasim Akram was nicknamed the "King of Swing". He played for the Pakistan international team for nearly 20 years, often as captain.

Akram was one of the best bowlers in the sport. He was known for his fast bowling style. By the end of his career, he had played in 460 international cricket matches and took a total of 916 wickets. This means that during his career, he was the bowler when 916 batsmen were knocked out.

Akram takes a wicket against England in a 1992 match. Pakistan won the match and the tournament.

The All Blacks are New Zealand's rugby squad. For 14 years, Richie McCaw was one of their best players. Throughout his career, McCaw had strength, speed and expert ball-handling skills.

McCaw played a total of 148 matches for New Zealand. The All Blacks won 131 of these matches. McCaw captained the team 110 times.

Richie McCaw and the All Blacks with the 2015 Rugby World Cup trophy. They beat Australia in the final.

He led New Zealand to ten Rugby
Championships and two World Cups.
McCaw was named World Rugby
Player of the Year three times.

McCaw retired from rugby in 2015.
He then achieved his lifelong dream
of becoming a helicopter pilot.

McCaw runs with the ball
as he dodges past defenders
from Georgia during the
2015 Rugby World Cup.

Young sports stars

Some sports stars are very successful at a young age – but only after spending a lot of time training.

Simone Biles

USA

Simone Biles has loved gymnastics since she was six years old. During her teens, she won five Olympic medals.

Lewis Hamilton

Britain

Lewis Hamilton was 16 when he started racing cars. He won his first Formula One Championship when he was 23.

Rory McIlroy

Britain

Golfer Rory McIlroy shot his first hole-in-one when he was nine. He became professional at age 18. McIlroy has won many golf tournaments.

Jessica Long

USA

So far, swimmer Jessica Long has won a total of 23 Paralympic medals. She won her first at just 12 years old.

Lionel Messi

Argentina

Lionel Messi became a professional football player at just 17. He's been FIFA Player of the Year five times.

Chapter 2
Sports on court

Many sports are played on courts, where space can be tight and play is quick. Billie Jean King was a star on the tennis court.

As a child, King saved up enough money to buy her first tennis racquet. She started playing professionally as a teenager. King was ranked world number one by 1966. During her career, King won 39 Grand Slams – the four most important tennis tournaments.

In 1973, King played against a man named Bobby Riggs. This tennis match was called the "Battle of the Sexes".

Even though Riggs was 55 years old, he thought he could beat the top female tennis players. King won, and her victory helped women's sports to be taken more seriously.

Billie Jean King playing a match at the Clairol Crown tennis tournament in 1980.

Wayne Gretzky's nickname is "The Great One". He is thought to be the best ice hockey player ever. From a young age, Gretzky spent many hours practising on a local ice rink in Canada. He became an expert at controlling and passing the hockey puck. This is the rubber disc that slides across the ice.

During his career in the National Hockey League (NHL), Gretzky broke many records. These include scoring a total of 894 goals.

Gretzky is the NHL's all-time leading goal scorer. He was named Most Valuable Player (MVP) eight times in a row, too.

Wayne Gretzky playing for the Edmonton Oilers in 1986. This match was against the Hartford Whalers.

Sporting great Martina Navratilova was a tennis champion from the 1970s to the 1990s. Serena Williams has had similar success. She has been ranked world number one for much of the last 20 years.

Williams and her four sisters played tennis as children. Now Williams has won more matches in major competitions than any other player. She has beaten Navratilova's record of 306 wins. So far Williams has won 23 Grand Slam singles titles and 14 Grand Slam doubles titles. She has also won four Olympic gold medals. Williams has won many of her doubles titles playing with her sister, Venus.

Serena Williams prepares to return a shot at the 2013 Mutua Open in Madrid. Williams won the tournament.

There are many legendary players in basketball. LeBron James is one of the greatest. He can jump incredibly high and has an accurate aim when shooting. James is 2.03 m (6 ft 8 in) tall. These qualities make him a star.

James has played in the National Basketball Association (NBA) since 2003. He often scores 27 points in a game, and more than 2,000 points in a season.

James playing for the Los Angeles Lakers. He heads towards the basket in a 2018 game against the Miami Heat.

He's been named MVP four times and played on three championship-winning teams. James has also won three Olympic medals with Team USA – two gold and one bronze.

Chinese table tennis great Ma Long keeps his opponents on their toes. He does this by staying on the attack.

Ma began to play table tennis when he was only five years old. At 15, he started playing for the Chinese national team. Ma has been ranked world number one many times.

Ma Long playing a match in the 2018 ITTF World Tour tournament in China.

In 2016, Ma won what is known as the "Golden Grand Slam". This means he won the World Championship, World Cup and three Olympic gold medals. In 2019, Ma won his 28th International Table Tennis Federation (ITTF) singles title. This is more times than any other player.

Netball player Irene van Dyk had great aim. She was thought to be the best goal shooter in the world. Van Dyk started playing netball in South Africa. She represented the national team 72 times. In 2000, she moved to New Zealand. She played in three World Cups for the Silver Ferns, New Zealand's national netball team.

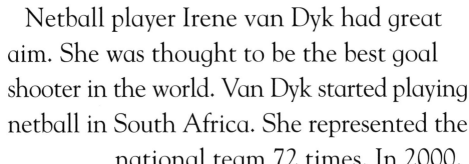

Irene van Dyk shoots in a match against Jamaica at the 2002 Commonwealth Games.

Goalkeeper Sharni Layton jumps to block a shot by the England netball team. This match was at the International Netball Series in 2016.

Sharni Layton is known for her strong defence skills and determination to win the ball. She was a star of Australia's national netball team and won two Netball World Cup gold medals. Layton was named Australian International Player of the Year in 2016. Layton retired from netball in 2018. She now plays Australian rules football.

Aim, attack and defend

Different skills are needed for different sports. Athletes are always training to improve their skills.

Kim Woo-jin, South Korea

Archer Kim Woo-jin has great aim. He usually hits the centre of the target. Woo-jin has won many archery medals, including at the 2016 Olympics.

Saori Yoshida, Japan

Wrestler Saori Yoshida attacks and defends as she tries to win a match. From 2002 to 2016, she won 13 world titles and three Olympic gold medals.

Valentina Vezzali, Italy

Valentina Vezzali needs to be good at attack and defence in fencing. Known for her speed and aim, she is nicknamed "The Cobra". Vezzali has won nine Olympic medals.

Chapter 3
Athletics

In athletics, there are many sporting greats. They are talented at running, jumping and throwing.

One of the greatest athletes of all time was Jesse Owens. In 1935, Owens set three new world records. His record long jump distance remained unbeaten for 25 years.

Owens won four gold medals for the USA at the 1936 Olympics in Nazi Germany. These were for the 100-metre sprint, 200-metre sprint, long jump and 4x100 metres relay race.

Hitler, the leader of Nazi Germany, believed the Olympics would show the world that German athletes were the best. However, Owens ran very fast and won the crowd over. The stadium erupted with cheers at his victories.

Jesse Owens running in the 200-metre sprint at the 1936 Olympic Games.

British wheelchair racer Tanni Grey-Thompson is one of the world's greatest Paralympic athletes. She was born with spina bifida, which affects a person's back. This means that she uses a wheelchair. From a young age, Grey-Thompson loved sports. At 13, she decided to focus on wheelchair racing.

Tanni Grey-Thompson wins gold at the 2004 Paralympic Games in Athens, Greece.

She joined the British Wheelchair Racing Squad at just 17 years old. From 1988 to 2004, Grey-Thompson won 16 Paralympic medals. These include 11 gold medals. She has also won the London Marathon six times. Grey-Thompson is now a member of the House of Lords (part of the British government).

Athlete Cathy Freeman was the favourite to win the 400-metre race at the 2000 Olympic Games. She is a proud Aboriginal Australian. Freeman had already won a silver medal at the 1996 Olympics. She had also won two world championships and three Commonwealth Games gold medals. But Freeman had always dreamt of winning an Olympic gold medal.

That year, the Olympics took place in Sydney, Australia. Freeman ran fast, worked hard and won the gold medal. She won with a time of just over 49 seconds. On her victory lap, she carried both the Australian and Aboriginal flags.

Cathy Freeman at the start of a 400-metre race at the 1996 Olympic Games.

Jessica Ennis-Hill throws the javelin at an athletics competition in England, in 2016.

The heptathlon is made up of seven track and field athletics events. Sports stars who do the heptathlon need to have many skills to be good at all of the events.

British athlete Jessica Ennis-Hill did the heptathlon. She won three world championships, an Olympic gold medal and an Olympic silver medal. Ennis-Hill won her gold medal in front of an excited home crowd at the 2012 London Olympics.

Athletics great Jackie Joyner-Kersee also did the heptathlon. This was during the 1980s and 1990s. Joyner-Kersee won a total of three Olympic gold medals, one silver medal and two bronze medals for the USA. She was the first athlete to score more than 7,000 points in total in a heptathlon.

Jackie Joyner-Kersee runs the 100-metre hurdles. This is one of the heptathlon events.

Jamaican superstar Usain Bolt is known as the world's fastest sprinter. At a height of 1.95 m (6 ft 5 in), he uses his long, powerful legs to run quickly. Bolt leaves his opponents far behind.

Usain Bolt after running in a 4x100-metre relay in 2011. The Jamaican team achieved a world record time of 36.84 seconds.

Bolt started breaking records as a teenager. He has since won a total of eight gold medals in the 100-metre and 200-metre races. He won these medals in three Olympic Games in 2008, 2012 and 2016. Bolt set new records in three races at the 2008 Olympics. These were the 100-metre, 200-metre and 4x100-metre relay.

Bolt doing his race-winning pose. It is widely known as the "lightning bolt".

Record breakers

Sporting greats love breaking records and doing something that no one has ever done before.

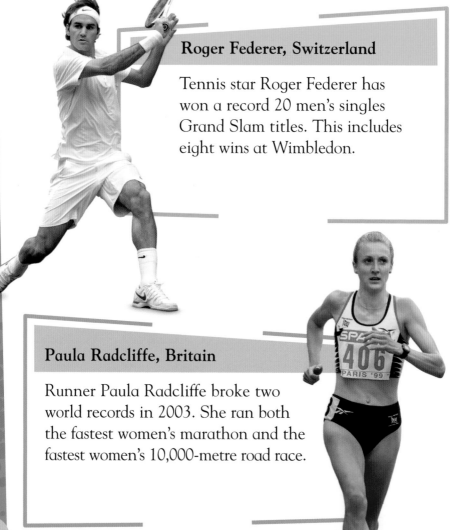

Roger Federer, Switzerland

Tennis star Roger Federer has won a record 20 men's singles Grand Slam titles. This includes eight wins at Wimbledon.

Paula Radcliffe, Britain

Runner Paula Radcliffe broke two world records in 2003. She ran both the fastest women's marathon and the fastest women's 10,000-metre road race.

Marit Bjørgen, Norway

Cross-country skier Marit Bjørgen holds the record for most medals won at the Winter Olympics. So far she has won 15 Olympic medals.

Mo Farah, Britain

Mo Farah won gold medals in the 5,000-metre and 10,000-metre races at two Olympic Games in a row. This record is known as a "double double".

Sachin Tendulkar, India

Cricket star Sachin Tendulkar holds many records. These include a total of 34,357 runs scored during international matches.

Chapter 4
Other sports

There are greats in many other sports, too. One of the all-time sporting greats was American boxer Muhammad Ali. Ali was quick on his feet. He liked to dance around the ring before throwing one of his mighty punches.

Muhammad Ali during a boxing match against Trevor Berbick in 1981.

Ali won a gold medal at the 1960 Olympics. He went on to become the world heavyweight champion three times. Two of his most well-known matches were the "Thriller in Manila" against Joe Frazier, and the "Rumble in the Jungle" against George Foreman. Ali won both matches, beating tough opponents.

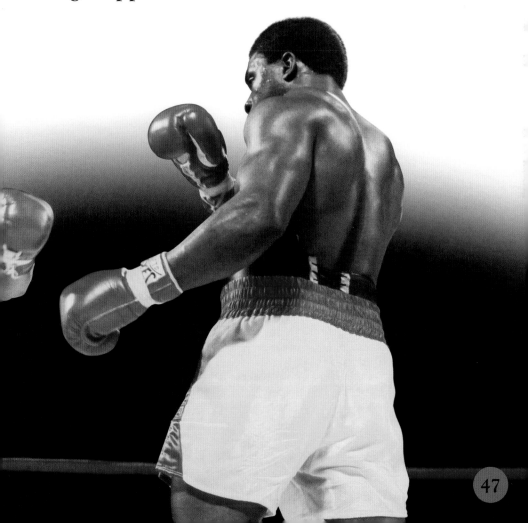

Nadia Comăneci was 14 when she became the first gymnast to receive a perfect score of 10 at the Olympic Games. The Romanian gymnast achieved seven perfect 10s at the 1976 Olympics. Comăneci won three gold medals, one silver medal and one bronze medal. At the 1980 Olympics, she won four more medals.

Nadia Comăneci performs on the balance beam in Japan, in 1979.

Gabby Douglas competing at the AT&T American Cup in 2016. She won gold.

Gabby Douglas's love of gymnastics began when her sister taught her to do a cartwheel when she was a child. She earned the nickname "Flying Squirrel" because she flies so high on the uneven bars. So far, Douglas has won three Olympic gold medals for the USA. She won two in 2012 and one in 2016.

Japanese judo superstar Ryoko Tani was World Judo Champion seven times. She also won a total of five Olympic medals. Tani started training in judo at just seven years old. Her talent and determination to win are huge.

Tani won silver medals at the 1992 and 1996 Olympics. However, she wanted to be the best. For 12 years, Tani was undefeated in international competition. She won her Olympic gold medals in 2000 and 2004, and a bronze medal in 2008.

Ryoko Tani beats an opponent. She won gold at the 2004 Olympic Games.

So far, British swimmer Ellie Simmonds has won eight Paralympic medals. These include five gold medals. Simmonds has dwarfism, which stops a person from growing very tall. She was only 13 when she won her first two gold medals at the 2008 Paralympics. In 2012, Simmonds achieved her first world record. This was in the 400-metre freestyle race.

Ellie Simmonds swims the butterfly stroke in a 200-metre race in 2019.

Michael Phelps celebrates winning the gold medal in the 100-metre butterfly race at the 2008 Olympics.

Michael Phelps is an American swimming superstar. His nickname is the "Flying Fish". Phelps started swimming as a child to use up extra energy. Now, he has won more Olympic medals than anyone else in history. Phelps has won a total of 23 gold, three silver and two bronze Olympic medals. Many people think he is the greatest swimmer of all time.

Laura Kenny in the lead during a race at the Revolution Track Series in London, in 2016.

Super-cyclist Laura Kenny has won four Olympic gold medals. Kenny was born with asthma, a health condition that makes breathing difficult. She was told that doing exercise would help. Her mother decided that the family should cycle together. But Kenny wanted to race, so she joined a cycling club.

Kenny and her husband, Jason, were part of the British cycling team that won 12 events at the 2012 Olympics. Kenny broke world records on her way to winning two gold medals. She won two more gold medals at the 2016 Olympics. Kenny's sporting career is not over yet!

Winter sports stars

Winter sports such as skiing, skating and sledding take place on snow and ice. Winter sports stars must be ready for the cold!

 Lindsey Vonn, USA

Lindsey Vonn has skied in downhill, slalom and other alpine ski races. She has won many races and has three Olympic medals.

 Surya Bonaly, France

At the 1998 Winter Olympics, figure skater Surya Bonaly did a backflip and landed on one skate. She was the first person to do this.

 Lizzy Yarnold, Britain

Lizzy Yarnold races down an icy track on a special type of sled called a skeleton. She won gold medals at the 2014 and 2018 Winter Olympics.

 Scott Moir and Tessa Virtue, Canada

Skating partners Scott Moir and Tessa Virtue won gold at the 2018 Winter Olympics. This added to their total haul of five Olympic medals.

Quiz

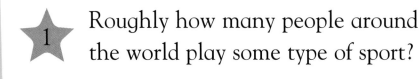

1   Roughly how many people around the world play some type of sport?

2   In what country did Ichiro Suzuki play baseball before moving to the USA?

3   How old was swimmer Jessica Long when she won her first Paralympic medal?

4   How many times in a row was Wayne Gretzky named MVP?

5   How tall is LeBron James?

6   What is Valentina Vezzali's nickname?

7 In what year did Jesse Owens win four Olympic gold medals?

 8 How many track and field events are in a heptathlon?

 9 Which races did Mo Farah win to achieve what is known as a "double double"?

 10 Nadia Comăneci was the first gymnast to achieve what score?

 11 In total, how many Olympic medals has Michael Phelps won?

 12 What type of sled does Lizzy Yarnold use in her races?

Answers on page 61

Glossary

Aboriginal and Torres Strait Islander peoples
The first people of Australia.

Australian rules football
A game that is similar to rugby and football.
It is played in Australia.

FIFA
The Fédération Internationale de Football
Association, the organization that makes the
rules of international football.

friendly match
A sports match that is played outside of a tournament,
played for either entertainment or practice.

heavyweight boxer
A boxer who weighs more than 79 kg (175 lbs). They
will only compete against other heavyweight boxers.

Nazi
A member of the National Socialist German Workers'
Party, which took control of Germany in 1933.

Olympic Games
An international sports competition, which is held
every four years.

opponent
The person or team who is playing against you.

Paralympic Games
An international sports competition for disabled athletes, which is held every four years.

rank
The level at which a sportsperson is considered to be, such as world number one.

relay race
A race that is run by a team, such as the 4x100-metre relay. Each member of the team runs part of the race.

run
A point scored in a game of cricket or baseball.

slalom
A type of skiing race where skiers have to ski in and out of flag posts in a zig-zag down a hill.

touchdown
The six points scored in American football when a team gets the ball over the opposition's goal line.

track and field events
Athletics events. Field events include the javelin and the long jump, and track events include running.

Answers to the quiz:
1. 600 million; 2. Japan; 3. 12 years old; 4. Eight; 5. 2.03 m (6 ft 8 in); 6. "The Cobra"; 7. 1936; 8. Seven; 9. 5,000-metre and 10,000-metre races; 10. A perfect 10; 11. 28 Olympic medals; 12. A skeleton sled

Index

A LEVEL FOR EVERY READER

This book is a part of an exciting four-level reading series to support children in developing the habit of reading widely for both pleasure and information. Each book is designed to develop a child's reading skills, fluency, grammar awareness and comprehension in order to build confidence and enjoyment when reading.

Ready for a Level 3 (Beginning to Read Alone) book
A child should:
- be able to read many words without needing to stop and break them down into sound parts.
- read smoothly, in phrases and with expression and at a good pace.
- self-correct when a word or sentence doesn't sound right or doesn't make sense.

A valuable and shared reading experience
For many children, reading requires much effort, but adult participation can make reading both fun and easier. Here are a few tips on how to use this book with a young reader:

Check out the contents together:
- read about the book on the back cover and talk about the contents page to help heighten interest and expectation.
- ask the reader to make predictions about what they think will happen next.
- talk about the information he/she might want to find out.

Encourage fluent reading:
- encourage reading aloud in fluent, expressive phrases, making full use of punctuation and thinking about the meaning; if helpful, choose a sentence to read aloud to help demonstrate reading with expression.

Praise, share and talk:
- notice if the reader is responding to the text by self-correcting and varying his/her voice.
- encourage the reader to recall specific details after each chapter.
- let him/her pick out interesting words and discuss what they mean.
- talk about what he/she found most interesting or important and show your own enthusiasm for the book.
- read the quiz at the end of the book and encourage the reader to answer the questions, if necessary, by turning back to the relevant pages to find the answers.